AMAZON REVIEWS EXPOSED

The Truth about Amazon Reviews

TIMO HOFSTEE

Copyright 2014

Onlinemoneyexplained.com

Table of Contents

Copyright

Introduction

As an author myself, and after having self-published several books, it is unavoidable that sooner or later you get confronted with the question: "How am I going to sell this book?"

If you follow the marketing and promotion strategies that you will find all over the internet and your book still doesn't sell, you might start asking yourself the question "Why doesn't my book sell"?

Then you start to explore Amazon reviews. Every author will confirm: The more (good) reviews you have, the more books you will sell.

The Amazon T&C's (*Terms & Conditions*) are clear and somewhat restrictive as to what is allowed and what is not. And, with a couple of exceptions, the message is "just wait for the reviews to come".

Now what happens if you don't "just get" those reviews you are waiting for? Because there is a financial interest, the same happens as with any other activity where there is money involved. Be it horse racing, poker games or book sales. When there is money to be made, people will become very inventive in creating all kinds of workarounds and tricks, to influence the system.

So a whole industry was created around fake reviews. You might say, "Ok. Fine. Everybody knows. So why write a book about it?"

At first sight it might seem all a bit obvious. Ok, you need good reviews, so you'll pay someone to create them. But if you think a bit deeper about it, many questions will occur to you.

What kind of cheats are there? How do they work? Do they give the desired results? Are there any drawbacks? How many fake reviews are there? Why doesn't Amazon do anything about it? And when you consider the question a bit further, you will come to the conclusion that fake reviews probably aren't the best way to influence sales.

When you start to dig a bit deeper into this issue you realize that there is a lot for you to learn. That's why I wrote this book.

Having said that, I'm not Robin Hood. I'm not a crusader against fake reviews. You have to decide for yourself whether or not you think fake reviews are acceptable or not. If there is anybody who should do something about this problem, then it is Amazon, right? But even that is not an obvious answer. You'll learn why as you read my book.

When I refer to a fake review that I have seen on Amazon as an example, I have changed some of the wording so that the review or the author cannot be traced back. I am not out to embarrass or accuse any authors. I don't agree with some of the methods they use, but they have to decide themselves what rules they want to break.

I'm in the fortunate position (at least for the moment) where I don't have to live from my book sales. And given my age (57), my "great career" aspirations are behind me. My book writing is a really a hobby, and one that I enjoy tremendously. I don't have any bestselling books so I have no reason to pull down any competitors.

I consider other authors fellow writers, rather than look at them as competitors even if we are writing in the same genre.

The idea for this book came after I read two books on Amazon reviews.

The first one was "How to get good reviews on Amazon" by Theo Rogers. This book explains in detail, and very honestly, what the whole Amazon review community is about. If you don't know about the Amazon reviewer culture I would recommend that book.

The second book, which I will not name in detail, explained how to get reviews by buying them. Because buying reviews is a real no-no for Amazon I decided to read this book to discover how well this cheating tactic would work for this author. You'll read about this later, but I can already tell you that it didn't make the bestsellers list...

The author of the second book also went as far as to boldly state in his book description that this was an 'Amazon approved system'. In the book itself, he refers to this "method" as an "ethical bribe". I did a search on Google what an ethical bribe is, but I haven't found any results. I don't think there is such a thing.

Who is this book for

I wrote this book for Amazon self-published authors and product sellers in any category . It will be of interest to anyone who sells on Amazon and who wants to learn about the different cheats that your competition may use. You'll also learn whether or not it is worth cheating.

Who is this book NOT for

If you are interested in the "nitty gritty" details about how various cheats work, then this book is NOT for you. Because I've never used any of these cheats myself, so all conclusions I have about their effectiveness is from other sellers and extensive research on the internet. I will tell you about the most common cheats. Some of these you may already know.

However, IF you have used some of the unethical strategies that I discuss in this book and you didn't get the expected results, you'll no doubt enjoy find out WHY they didn't work.

The Amazon review system

Before going into the meat of fake reviews, let's try to get a better understanding about what we're talking about, by analyzing some data.

How many Kindle eBooks are there? About 2,7 million titles. This is easy to lookup on the Amazon Kindle store.

Although we don't know exactly how the Amazon Bestsellers Rank is calculated, by cross checking data from different authors it is possible to recreate an approximate table with sales rank versus daily sales.

I have published one in my book 'The Ultimate Kindle Marketing Guide', but you can also look it up on my blog over here.

http://www.onlinemoneyexplained.com/what-is-amazon-best-sellers-rank/

These are the first two columns in the following table.

From that data we can construct the following table:

Rank	Estimated daily sales	nr of titles	daily volume	cumul volume	% of total volume	cum% of total volume	%of titles	cum% of titles
1-5	5 000	5	25 000	25 000	1.47%	1.47%	0.0002%	0.0002%
5-20	4 000	15	60 000	85 000	3.53%	5.00%	0.0005%	0.0007%
20-40	3 000	20	60 000	145 000	3.53%	8.54%	0.0007%	0.0013%
40-80	2 500	40	100 000	245 000	5.89%	14.42%	0.0013%	0.0027%
80-150	2 000	70	140 000	385 000	8.24%	22.66%	0.0023%	0.0050%
150-300	500	150	75 000	460 000	4.42%	27.08%	0.0050%	0.0100%
300-500	250	200	50 000	510 000	2.94%	30.02%	0.0067%	0.0167%
500-750	175	250	43 750	553 750	2.58%	32.60%	0.0083%	0.0250%
750-1.500	120	750	90 000	643 750	5.30%	37.90%	0.0250%	0.0500%
1.500-3.000	100	1 500	150 000	793 750	8.83%	46.73%	0.0500%	0.1000%
3.000-5.000	70	2 000	140 000	933 750	8.24%	54.97%	0.0667%	0.1667%
5.000-10.000	25	5 000	125 000	1 058 750	7.36%	62.33%	0.1667%	0.3333%
10.000-20.000	15	10 000	150 000	1 208 750	8.83%	71.16%	0.3333%	0.6667%
20.0000-50.000	5	30 000	150 000	1 358 750	8.83%	79.99%	1.0000%	1.6667%
50.000-100.000	1	50 000	50 000	1 408 750	2.94%	82.93%	1.6667%	3.3333%
100.000-2.700.000	0.1	2 900 000	290 000	1 698 750	17.07%	100.00%	96.6667%	100.0000%

Now if we plot the Rank against the cumulative percentage of total sales volume and against cumulative percentage of titles, we get the following chart:

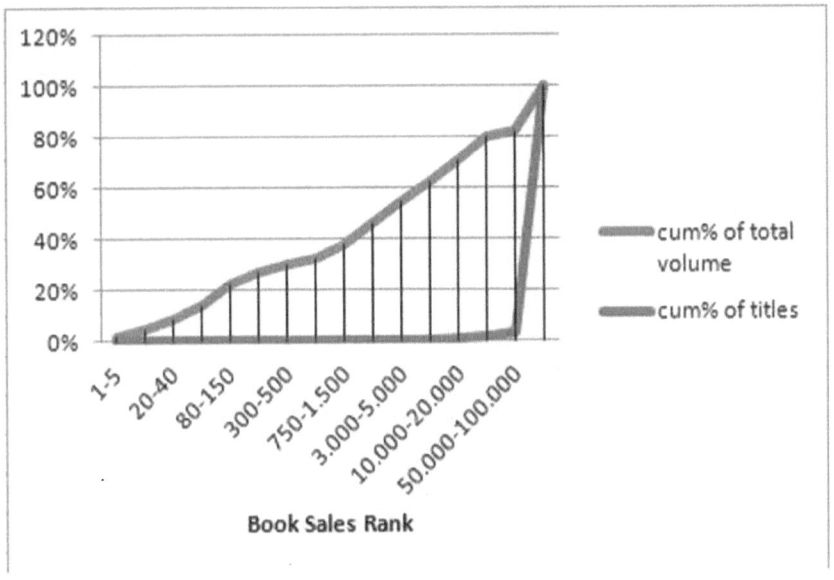

What does this chart tell us?

- 50% of the sales volume is made with the top 0,16% of the titles.

- 80% of the sales volume is made with approximately the top 3% of the titles.

- This means that the remaining 20% of sales is distributed over the 97% of the remaining titles.

- These 97% of the titles sell less than 1 book a day. A good part of this 97% sells zero.

This means that the probability of having a book in the top 100 is very small. Believe it or not, a book that sells (on average) 2 copies a day ranks already in the top 2%.

A study on the top 500 list (2013) reveals that only 700 indie authors are earning more than 25.000$ a year. So if your book, which will start as just one of the 2.7 million books on Amazon, ends up in the top 0.025%, you can start make a full-time income from your writing activities. You can find the full report here.

http://authorearnings.com/the-tenured-vs-debut-author-report/

Some people might say that these figures are a bit skewed, because a lot of titles are just 'dead' stock. And indeed, of the 2.7 million titles we can assume that only the top 500.000 sell. All the rest are books that sell nothing or maybe a couple of copies a year.

Some of these books were published years ago and never made any sales. Or they may have sold only a few copies. They might have been abandoned by the author. If we ignore everything in the table above but the top 500.000, does that change a lot? The table would now look like this:

Rank	Estimated daily sales	nr of titles	daily volume	cumul volume	% of total volume	cum% of total volume	%of titles	cum% of titles
1-5	5 000	5	25 000	25 000	1.73%	1.73%	0.0010%	0.0010%
5-20	4 000	15	60 000	85 000	4.14%	5.87%	0.0030%	0.0040%
20-40	3 000	20	60 000	145 000	4.14%	10.01%	0.0040%	0.0080%
40-80	2 500	40	100 000	245 000	6.90%	16.91%	0.0080%	0.0160%
80-150	2 000	70	140 000	385 000	9.66%	26.57%	0.0140%	0.0300%
150-300	500	150	75 000	460 000	5.18%	31.75%	0.0300%	0.0600%
300-500	250	200	50 000	510 000	3.45%	35.20%	0.0400%	0.1000%
500-750	175	250	43 750	553 750	3.02%	38.22%	0.0500%	0.1500%
750-1.500	120	750	90 000	643 750	6.21%	44.43%	0.1500%	0.3000%
1.500-3.000	100	1 500	150 000	793 750	10.35%	54.79%	0.3000%	0.6000%
3.000-5.000	70	2 000	140 000	933 750	9.66%	64.45%	0.4000%	1.0000%
5.000-10.000	25	5 000	125 000	1 058 750	8.63%	73.08%	1.0000%	2.0000%
10.000-20.000	15	10 000	150 000	1 208 750	10.35%	83.43%	2.0000%	4.0000%
20.0000-50.000	5	30 000	150 000	1 358 750	10.35%	93.79%	6.0000%	10.0000%
50.000-100.000	1	50 000	50 000	1 408 750	3.45%	97.24%	10.0000%	20.0000%
100.000-500.000	0.1	400 000	40 000	1 448 750	2.76%	100.00%	80.0000%	100.0000%

And the chart like this

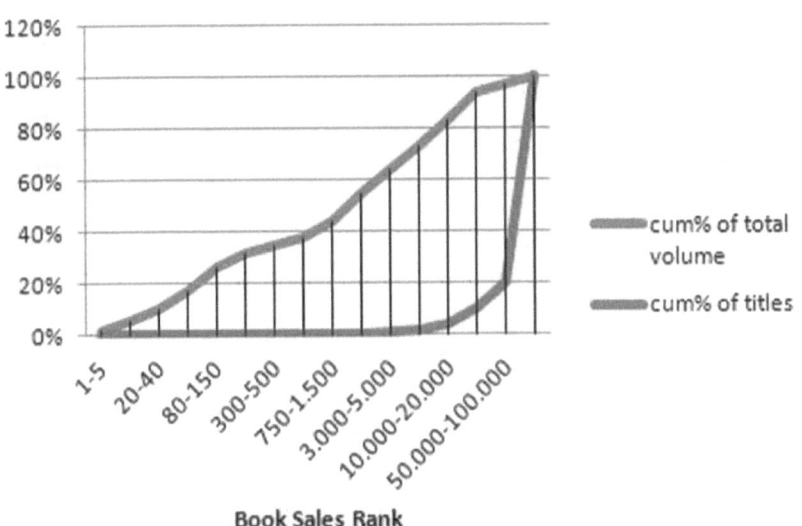

cum% of total volume

cum% of titles

Book Sales Rank

And indeed, the results are slightly better. But not a lot. 83% of the sales still make up 4% of all the titles.

The good news is, that you can publish as many books as you want. But from the above we can conclude that if you have a book that sells 1-2 copies a day (30-60 monthly), you are doing already rather well. So if you want to make a living from writing books, then there is only one solution: write a lot of books.

How many should you write? Let's say you want to make 6000$/month and you make $2 profit on a book. That corresponds roughly with 100 sales/day. So if you want to make a living with books that sell 2 copies a day, you know how many books you have to write.

Don't forget that the 6000$ mentioned is gross income. And depending on the country you live in, you may have to pay 20-50% income tax on that. :(

Is there a relationship between reviews and sales rank?

Here is a scatter chart of the top 100 sales on Amazon (2013). It shows Sales Rank versus nr of reviews.

(source http://dodecahedronbooks.blogspot.fr/2014/01/amazon-top-100-kindle-books.html)

Now I will not bother you with all kind of statistical analysis and other complicated math. But this graph shows that there is a strong relationship between nr of reviews and sales rank.

The average is 1 review on 100 sales. So 1%. The deviation can be rather large. As the graph shows for some titles the nr of reviews is far more than expected and for others far less.

But they all fit within 2 limits : 0,5% and 1,5%. So this means that a low estimate is 1 review for 66 sales and a high estimate is 1 review for 200 sales. The average is 1 on 100. These figures become more and more unreliable when the number of reviews decreases.

Why is the difference so big? We call this engagement. For example, the price of the book. When someone buys a high priced book, they will be more inclined to leave a review. On the opposite side, on low priced books, buyers will feel less engaged and will most likely leave fewer reviews.

How important are reviews?

You could ask the question: Are reviews important? Wouldn't just any ranking whether a one or five-star review be enough? The answer has been proven over and over again. Figleaves.com increased sales by 35% when they introduced customer reviews. The reason is simple. Customer reviews act as the word-of-mouth message to potential buyers. And there is no stronger advertising than word-of-mouth. If your friend talks positively to you about a specific product, that message is usually more effective than all the marketing blurbs and reviews you might see put together.

How do reviews influence sales?

We already saw that there is a relationship between reviews and sales. But also that there was a considerable spread. When do reviews help most to boost your sales?

A team of researchers gathered data for 590 books from Amazon, including their reviews and analyzed factors, such as price and review volume to see their influence on conversion rate and sales.

It came as no surprise that negative reviews have much more impact than positive ones. What was more surprising was, that having a large number of reviews, regardless of their contents, had a positive impact on sales!

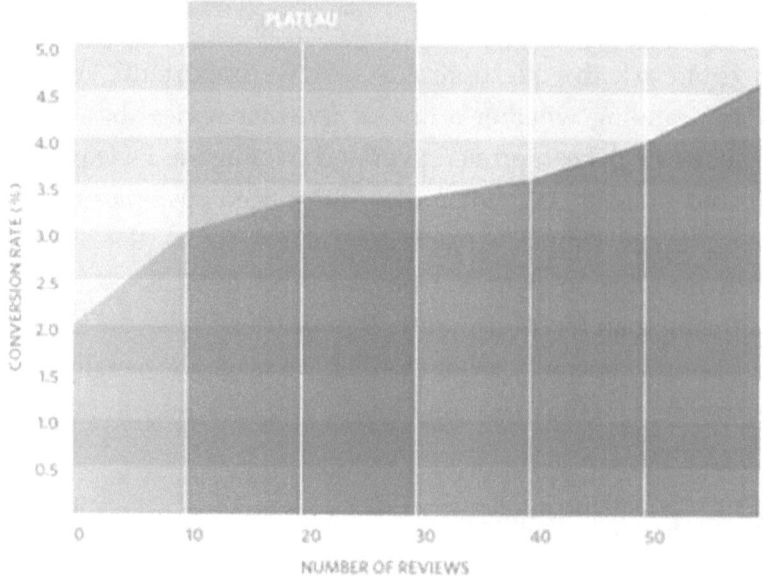

This graph shows the relationship between nr of reviews and conversion rate. The slope of the graph shows the positive effect on conversion rate. So we see that the slope is the steepest from 0-10 reviews. This means that the first 10 reviews have the biggest impact on sales. Around 20, the graph levels off. So sales will not significantly be better with 30 reviews than with 20.

Then the graph goes up again in an almost linear way. Which means: The more reviews there are, the higher the conversion rate. (And therefore the more sales).

The study also showed that the positive star rating didn't influence sales, but rather the content of the reviews. This is also easy to explain, because everybody has a different definition of 1,3 or 5 stars.

However, the study also found that the differentiation (or the variability) in star ratings DID influence sales. Books with lots of 5-star, some 4-star and a couple of 3 star ratings sold better than books with all 5-stars.

16

When customers see too many 5-star reviews, they get suspicious. Especially when they are all raving reviews.

How many reviews are there on Amazon?

That's a very difficult question. But we can get a rough estimate for it. On Amazon US, there are 245 million references. All products included. On all the other Amazon sites (.de, .it, .fr, .uk etc.) there are another 650 million references. Each with their own reviews. That's almost 900 million references!!

If we assume an average of 5 reviews per reference, we get close to 5 billion reviews. But whatever the number is, it is HUGE.

How many reviews are posted on Amazon daily?

Again, very difficult to answer, but we can make again a rough estimate. During Christmas run-up, Amazon worldwide was selling 426 items per second. So if we assume that a 'normal' average rate is 100 items per second, that makes 8.6 million items per day.

And if we assume one review on every 100 items sold, that makes 86000 reviews a day.

This explains immediately why it is impossible to verify all reviews by human beings.

Why do people use fake reviews ?

Now that we have determined that there is a relationship between nr of reviews and sales (and therefore financial gain), we also have established the reason why certain people will use fake reviews.

As we have seen, especially the first 10-20 reviews are important.

But what is a fake review? The definition that I will use in this book is: **Any review that isn't allowed according to the Amazon Terms & Conditions.**

What do the Amazon T&C's say about reviews?

"Promotional content:

• Advertisements, promotional material or repeated posts that make the same point excessively

*• Sentiments by or on behalf of a person or company **with a financial interest in the product** or a directly competing product (including reviews by publishers, manufacturers, or third-party merchants selling the product)*

*• Reviews written **for any form of compensation** other than a free copy of the product. This includes reviews that are a part of a paid publicity package*

*• **Solicitations for helpful votes***

Inappropriate content:

*• **Other people's material** (this includes excessive quoting)*

• Phone numbers, postal mailing addresses, and URLs external to Amazon.com

• Videos with watermarks

- *Comments on other reviews visible on the page (because page visibility is subject to change without notice)*
- *Foreign language content*

*We have a **zero tolerance policy** for any review designed to mislead or manipulate customers.*

If you have a direct or indirect financial interest in a product, or perceived to have a close personal relationship with its author or artist, we'll likely remove your review.

Here are a few examples of reviews that we don't allow:

-A product manufacturer posts a review of their own product, posing as an unbiased shopper.

-A shopper, unhappy with her purchase, posts multiple negative reviews for the same product.

-A customer posts a review in exchange for $5.

*-a **family member of the product creator posts a five-star customer review to help boost sales**.*

-A shopper posts a review of the product, after being promised a refund in exchange.

-A seller posts negative reviews on his competitor's product

-An artist posts a positive review on a peer's album in exchange for receiving a positive review from them"

That sums it up pretty well. To put it the other way around, what is permitted?

- Just wait for the reviews

- Distribute free copies and ask for an honest review.

Fake reviews can lead to large financial gain. And the risks are relatively low. I don't know what Amazon's sanctions are for the different kinds of fraud. It is for sure that shill accounts and fake reviews are deleted as soon as they are signaled (and proven to be a fake). However, I have never read anywhere about an author account being closed because of fraud. Worst I have seen is that an account gets suspended for an undetermined period of time.

Some authors do argue in length in forums and on blogs, if these rules make sense or not. And why fake reviews aren't that bad, why buying reviews is not a big issue, etc.

My stake on this is : These are the rules. You may like them or not, you may agree with them or not, but we are using Amazon's site for our products. And Amazon can do on their site whatever they want. And put the rules as they want.

If authors start arguing : "Well, I don't agree with rule X, and I don't consider that a fraud", than Amazon should just simply cancel all their rules. Because if every author gives its own interpretation to the rules then what's the point.

Would a review system without ANY rules work? Well, that would be a bit similar to abandoning the 'rule' in society that you have to pay for what is in your basket when you leave a shop. As in real life , a society cannot operate without establishing certain rules. And any online voting system will need certain rules.

So if we agree that Amazon has to put some rules in place to level the playing ground for everybody, we still could argue if the rules that they have defined are 'reasonable' or not.

For example, in my research, I read about cases where Amazon removed reviews because there was a 'link' between the author and the person that wrote the review. One of these cases went like this : The author ordered an item (not a book) on Amazon and had it shipped to his mother in another state in the US. Later on, when the author published his book, his mother left a review.

The review was removed by Amazon, because they considered that there was a 'link' between the author and the person that left the review. Fair?

I don't know. That's up to Amazon to decide. But apparently they do have some mechanism in place to detect if there is a relationship between an author and a reviewer.

How many fake reviews are there?

When I started my research for this book, I only had my own opinion and my own experience after reading hundreds of reviews. And from my point of view, the number was rather considerable. I would have guessed somewhere around 10% of the ones I read.

But when I started to search for articles and blogs dealing with the issue, I found tons and tons of references to supposedly fake reviews and suspicious authors.

According to different sources, the estimates go anywhere from 10% to 60%. In the fiverr report (http://five-report.blogspot.fr/) it is mentioned that , according to an ex Amazon employee, Amazon's own internal memorandums mention a fraud rate of 60%. This includes bought , traded , swapped or any other kind of unethical behavior.

In my research I haven't found any evidence that prove or disqualify these numbers.

Notice that the above mentioned report doesn't disclose any of its sources and not even the author of the report. So I cannot confirm the accuracy of the content of that report.

How to get honest reviews?

From the Amazon site :

"Who can write Amazon.com customer reviews?

Anyone registered as an Amazon.com customer and who has made at least one purchase for ANY product is entitled to write customer reviews.

Does the reviewer have to buy the item from Amazon.com?

No. It doesn't matter where an item was purchased, or if it was a gift, or if the reviewer just borrowed it for a weekend. If someone feels moved to write a review of an item, and they are a registered Amazon.com customer, they are welcome."

There are several ways to get honest reviews. The best, and most obvious way is: write a good book. If your book is good, it WILL get reviews.

Another way is, to post a request on book review sites, asking if anybody would like to review your book. Notice that when you do this, you are very likely getting contacted by people that will propose you a review swap. Which is not allowed, according to the T&C's.

Book review websites

There are a couple of sites where you can publish your book and people will read them and give a review. You can then use these reviews in the front matter of your book or in the book description. Note that if you give exclusivity to Amazon for your book, you should do all this BEFORE you submit your book to Amazon.

Because if you give exclusivity to Amazon, you may not give away your book on ANY other site. So don't forget to take these down as soon as you publish.

* https://readersfavorite.com/

* http://www.stepbystepselfpublishing.net/reviewer-list.html . On this (long) list you will see all kinds of sites that publish reviews of books.

* https://www.faceBook.com/groups/reviewseekers/

* http://www.booklistonline.com/

* http://www.goodreads.com

Another way to go about this, is to first publish your book on Amazon, and then start looking for reviews. When someone wants to review your book, you send them a free copy and the reviewer can leave his/her review directly on the Amazon site.

You can also send them your book as a gift. Yes, that will cost you the 30% commission (if you're in the 70% royalty bracket). But at least these reviews will be accounted for as real sales.

Amazon reviewers

Another way to get objective reviews, is to solicit an Amazon reviewer. Amazon reviewers are people who review books as a hobby. So they are not paid for making reviews.

Amazon reviewers take their reviews very serious. There is a whole subculture around the Amazon reviewers, with their own forum, reviewer rankings and ethics. No it is not a sect. These are normal people like you and me. But I suggest that you read a bit about what drives Amazon reviewers before you approach one of them. Be polite and patient.

Amazon reviewers are ranked, according to the number and quality of their reviews. You can find the list of Amazon reviewers here:

http://www.amazon.com/review/top-reviewers

How to find an Amazon reviewer? Look through the reviews that have been given on books in your genre or competing books. Verify if any reviews are given by an Amazon reviewer. Not all reviewers leave their contact details. So you will have to scan through the Amazon reviewer pages to see if you can find the contact details for an Amazon reviewer.

The author marketing club has a tool that does this work for you, but you have to become a member of the club to be able to use that tool.

It is obvious that, the higher a reviewer gets into the Amazon reviewer ranking, the more these reviewers are solicited. And the top reviewers are probably inundated by review requests. So don't despair if you don't get an answer on your request. Just ask another reviewer who is sincerely interested in reviewing your book.

Note that an Amazon reviewer will leave you an objective and honest review. So you may expect that the review will correspond with the quality of your book, which may not correspond with what you expected.

If you want to know more about Amazon reviewer rankings, you can find it here.

http://www.amazon.com/review/guidelines/top-reviewers.html/

For more detailed information about the Amazon reviewer system, read the book from Theo Rogers that I mentioned in the beginning of this book.

If you want to know more about what drives Amazon reviewers you can find a study report that was published in 2011 here. 'A study of the Top 1000 customer reviewers at Amazon.com'.

https://docs.google.com/viewer?a=v&pid=sites&srcid=ZnJlZW x1bmNoLm1lfHRlc3R8Z3g6NDg0MjliMjM3OWQzMWRlNw

Ask for reviews

There is nothing wrong with asking your readers at the end of your book for an honest review. What is not allowed, is asking for a review and promising the reader any kind of compensation, like a refund, your next book free or whatever other reward.

Fake review tactics

In this chapter I will go through a number of tactics that are used by people to create fake or non-compliant reviews.

Reviews by family and friends

Although I wouldn't call these fake reviews, they are not allowed according to the T&C's. Why not? Because if your mother, sister or brother writes a review, by definition, it cannot be objective because that person knows the author. And I cannot imagine that a mother leaves a review on the first book of her son like :"I didn't understand anything in this book" with a 1 or 2-star rating.

So don't solicit friends and family to review your books. I have seen numerous postings in forums where people write :"my mum/friend left a review but it doesn't show up on Amazon".

This means that Amazon has put in place certain verifications to judge if your review has been posted by friends or family. I don't know the details, but there are some obvious ones. When you register, or when you write a review, Amazon knows your IP address. So if your spouse posts a review from her own account on your PC, that is an easy giveaway.

Also if reviewers have the same name, or live in the same neighborhood, their reviews are very likely to be eliminated.

Multiple accounts

This is probably the tactic that is used most, although I have no figures whatsoever to prove that. This tactic uses a so called shill. What is a shill? Here is the definition from Wikipedia:

*"A **shill**, also called a **plant** or a **stooge**, is a person who publicly helps a person or organization without disclosing that they have a close relationship with the person or organization.*

"Shill" typically refers to someone who purposely gives onlookers the impression that they are an enthusiastic independent customer of a seller (or marketer of ideas) for whom they are secretly working. The person or group who hires the shill is using crowd psychology to encourage other onlookers or audience members to purchase the goods or services (or accept the ideas being marketed). Shills are often employed by professional marketing campaigns. "Plant" and "stooge" more commonly refer to any person who is secretly in league with another person or organization while pretending to be neutral or actually a part of the organization he is planted in, such as a magician's audience, a political party, or an intelligence organization.

In online discussion media, satisfied consumers or "innocent" parties may express specific opinions in order to further the interests of an organization in which they have an interest, such as a commercial vendor or special interest group. In academia, this is called opinion spamming. Web sites can also be set up for the same purpose. For example, an employee of a company that produces a specific product might praise the product anonymously in a discussion forum or group in order to generate interest in that product, service, or group. In addition, some shills use "sock puppetry", where they sign on as one user soliciting recommendations for a specific product or service. They then sign on as a different user pretending to be a satisfied customer of a specific company."

So, the tactic is to create multiple accounts where the author leaves positive reviews on his own books. Or the author writes his own reviews and asks friends or family to post these under accounts that are created for that purpose.

Very often, these shills are relatively easy to detect, because these reviews look more like a sales letter, rather than an objective review.

The review swap

This is the tactic where author A leaves a review on a book from author B and author B leaves a review on a book from author A in return.

Although this sounds relatively simple to detect, just by cross checking the reviews and looking for example at the review date, in practice this is not that obvious. Take the example where author A , who writes romance novels, leaves a review on a book from another romance novel writer and the other way around. And in a time frame of a couple of days. Shill or not?

That's pretty hard to prove. And it may be very well a sincere review from each of them, without there having been any agreement on a swap.

Now let's take a more excessive example. Male author A leaves a 5-star rating on a book about PMS (premenstrual syndrome) written by female author B, and author B leaves a 5-star review on a book about body building from author A. And that, within a couple of days. Shill or not?

It looks a lot like it. But again, it MAY be just a matter of circumstances and author A bought the bought about PMS for his wife and author B bought the book about body building for her husband. Unlikely, but possible.

This shows that eliminating these cheats is not as easy as it sounds from Amazon's point of view.

Some authors argue: "what's wrong with exchanging honest reviews with another author? I give him/her my book for free and I leave an honest review, and the other author does the same. So it is within the Amazon T&C's".

Well, the problem is, that this does fall under the "no compensation rule" from Amazon. And let's face it. If you read a book from an author and you really don't like the book, would you give it a 1 or 2-star rating, knowing that the author is going to give your book also a rating?

Although I haven't done any deep research into this, the obvious review swaps that I have seen are ALL 4 or 5-star reviews. For obvious reasons.

The review circle

Review circles are an advanced version of the review swap. This is where for example 4 authors A,B,C and D swap reviews between each other. A leaves a review for B, B for C, C for D and D for A.

The purpose here is, to make it much more difficult for an outsider to detect the swap, because you now have to check 4 levels deep through the reviews.

The lottery

This tactic works as follows: The author puts his book up for sale for 0.99$ (or even free). He then promotes his book widely, asking people to buy/download his book and leave a positive review on his book. This, for a predefined period, for example one week. In exchange, the buyer will participate in a lottery where the author promises a 200$ item to the winner, who will be drawn randomly between the people who left a review.

This is clearly a bribe, because the author 'buys' his reviews. This scheme is particularly vicious because, when the buyer clicks on the link to buy the book, he first gets redirected to a landing page where he has to leave his email, and from there he is redirected to Amazon.

So the author builds his list at the same time that he is bribing readers for reviews.

I have seen a couple of books being promoted this way. And I have analyzed their results. And without going into details, the outcome is in all cases negative for the author.

Besides that, organizing online lotteries is very regulated in most countries and states in the US and in most of the cases strictly forbidden without the appropriate authorizations.

Buying reviews

Although the previous tactic described a tactic for indirectly buying reviews, there are people that go one step further. If you search on Google for 'book reviewer' or 'Amazon book reviewer', you will get a whole list of sites where people propose their review services for a 'modest' financial compensation.

Of course, this is strictly forbidden by the Amazon T&C's for obvious reasons. I cannot skip this issue, without talking about one of the most famous 'review buys' in recent eBook history. And I'm talking about the John Locke case.

I'm not revealing any secrets here, because this story created a major buzz in 2012. Here is the story in short.

Near the end of 2010, Mr. Rutherford got the bright idea that there was money to be made in selling reviews. And created the site gettingbookreviews.com .

The site was quickly a success, despite all the complaints in online forums about the ethics of this business.

Mr. Locke started his writing career in 2009 after a career in insurance and real estate. In the first months of his writing career he only sold a couple of thousand copies. Then suddenly, end of 2010, his sales started to spike in a spectacular way. Mid 2011, Mr. Locke had published nine novels and was the first author to achieve sales of 1 million books on Amazon.

In June 2011, Mr. Locke published his book "How I Sold 1 Million eBooks in 5 Months". What Mr. Locke didn't tell in his book, is that in October 2010 he ordered his first batch of 50 reviews from Mr. Rutherford for $1000.

And because the effect on his sales were very positive, he continued and bought in total over 300 reviews for Amazon and another 700 that were used on other sites like Goodreads and B&N. In all, over 1000 reviews.

Due to the sudden spectacular increase of positive reviews on his account, Amazon investigated his case and decided to remove most of Mr. Rutherfords bought reviews. The account of Mr. Locke took a hit, but wasn't closed.

Over the last years, fraud with fake accounts has exploded according to the site Zon Alert.

(http://zonalert.wordpress.com/).

According to the articles on this site, there are currently dozens and dozens of authors who are buying reviews by the truckload, and creating fake accounts by the thousands. They even have a 'Thumbs Down Author List' which lists the authors with the largest number of complaints.

This goes from sockpuppets to paid reviews, and from review swaps to fake fans and complete fake fan clubs.

Some authors have gone as far as creating complete pyramid schemes with other fraudulent authors. New recruits benefit from fake reviews from the top and the top of the pyramid benefits from all the fake reviews at the bottom of the pyramid.

Banging the competition

Another type of fake review is the 'bang the competition' type of reviews. These reviews go something like : 'I have read a lot of books on this subject and this one wasn't really very good. I prefer the books from author XYZ'.

Not only is this type of review not allowed according to the Amazon T&C's, but they also contain a clear giveaway that it is posted by author XYZ.

In this context it is worthwhile to mention that there is a specific naming for these kind of persons. They are called trolls. Trolls make outrageous claims and have only one objective: create online stir by writing extremely hurtful and negative reviews.

Buying your own books

This tactic is not specifically used to create fake reviews, but more to boost the sales rank of a book. Note that the Amazon Best Seller Rank is calculated only by sales and not by reviews.

This strategy is similar to the review circle. Let's say 20 authors group together. Every author buys the 19 books from the other authors. This assumes that all books are more or less priced the same. Now every author has spent 19 purchases, but in exchange he also makes 19 sales of his own book. Yes, every author will lose the 30% royalty that Amazon keeps. So if we assume a retail price of $3, every author will lose $17,10.

Now notice that in a lot of sub categories it is enough to make just a couple of sales a day to get to #1 in that subcategory. Obviously this tactic needs some coordination and planning. The whole purpose of the fraud is, to get a book to #1 in a sub category, therefore boosting exposure and therefore increasing sales that will pay back the small investment.

Note that there is nothing wrong with giving your book as a gift. Every book that you give away (and have paid for), will be counted as a regular sale as soon as the receiver of the gift redeems the gift voucher.

Why isn't Amazon doing anything about it ?

In several forums, where people complain about fake reviews, frequently the question comes up: Why doesn't Amazon do something about it.

The best way to get an answer to that question is, to ask Amazon. So I wrote to Amazon, asking them their feedback on the issues mentioned in this book. But as expected, I got a quick reply back, stating that I always could send them feedback on specific reviews but that they cannot disclose the results of their investigations. And honestly, I hadn't expected otherwise.

So we have to do some guessing on what is going on behind the screens.

Now I think there are two main reasons why Amazon isn't really handling this issue as we wish they were.

The first one is mainly technical. According to research that has been done, human beings aren't good in detecting fake reviews. It really takes some experience. But there are some cases where the shill seems very obvious. Unfortunately, the catch is in the word 'seems'.

Let's take the case where an author gets 15 five star reviews the same day, by the same person on 15 different books from the same author. Now this smells VERY much as a shill. But.... one COULD argue that that person has bought these 15 books over a period of a couple of weeks, and decided to handle all his reviews when he had read them all. Unlikely, but possible.

Or let's take a typical shill. Because when you read a lot of reviews, you start to get an eye for the way they are written. I give an example :

'John ABC did it again. This book is really awful. It explains in detail :

-how to XXX
-The way you can get XYZ
-5 reasons why you should ABC
-10 secrets how to achieve ZZZ

I applied these methods and the results have really been amazing. I've never read a book that was as clear and precise as the one written by John ABC'

Now the non-observing casual reader will maybe not immediately see what is wrong with this review. But if you read hundreds of reviews, you start to see similarities in the fake ones.

First of all, lots of the authors use their full name (first + last) in the review. And if possible, several times. As if they want to make sure that their name gets mentioned as often as possible. Now I don't write a lot of reviews myself, but IF I were to write a review, I would say something like : 'The author' or 'This book is..' or 'Mr ABC '. But I would rarely use the full name and even less , mentioning it 4 or 5 times in the same review.

The second giveaway is, that the 'reviewer' cites on the top of his head the complete contents of the book.

The third giveaway is that the review is full of exuberant words like 'awful', 'absolutely great', 'the best I've read in my life' , 'extraordinary', 'life changing' etc.etc. The review looks more like a sales letter, rather than an objective review.

But.....again, one COULD argue that this is a really satisfied customer who has written this review.

The fourth giveaway is that these self-published reviews are always pretty lengthy. At least 5 to 10 lines.

The fifth giveaway for a self-published review is, that the words, expressions and style of the review are very similar to the words and style used in the actual book. If I had to give one advice to anyone that is going to create fake reviews : Don't write them yourself. It is very difficult to write dozens and dozens of fake reviews without exposing your own writing style.

Let's take a look at the most classic example of a shill. This is the 5 star review given by someone who has given only 1 review in total on the same day that a book is published. And often , if you see this, there are several shills like that on the same day for the same book. This is a clear giveaway for a shill.

But.... again, one COULD argue that 'by accident', 10 readers got this book on the day of publishing and, although they have never given any review, all 10 of them felt urged to give this book a 5-star review the same day. Again, possible, but unlikely. But hard to prove.

Another indicator for fake reviews is the so called J-curve. In 2013 a study was done on the reviews of the top 20 NYT bestseller list. We may suppose that these highly successful authors have other things to deal with than creating fake reviews. For every book the number of 1,2,3,4 and 5 stars was calculated and surprisingly, all books had approximately the same percentages of 1-5 ratings. These percentages were:

1* : 9%

2 *: 5%

3* : 9%

4* : 18%

5*: 59%

If we plot this in a chart, we get :

% of total reviews

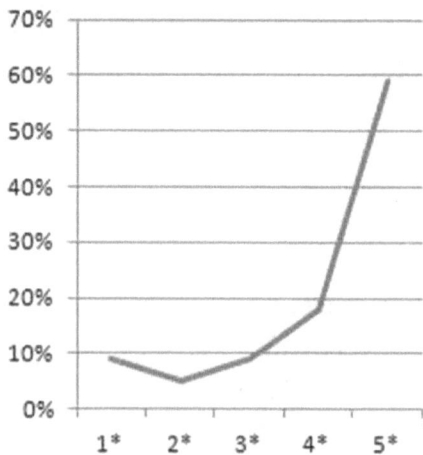

With a bit of imagination we can see the letter J in this chart. I verified this with the top 10 bestsellers on Amazon which had at least 1000 reviews.

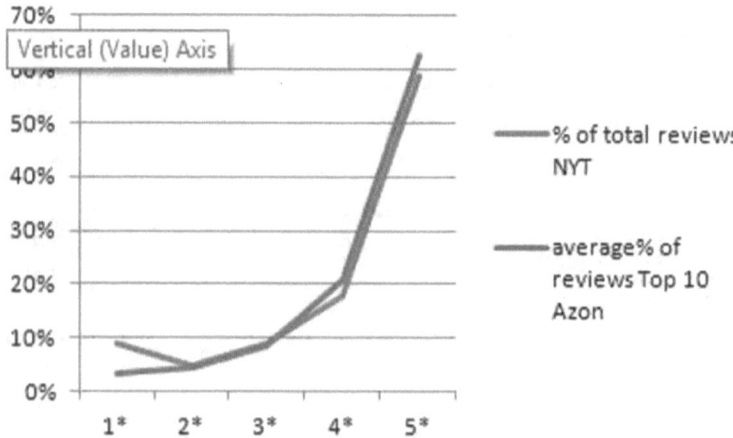

We see that the figures are lined up rather well, except for the 1* reviews which are around the 4% mark. 1* and 2* ratings together are around 8%. Apparently, Amazon readers are a bit less severe when it comes to 1* and 2* ratings.

I then took 10 books from an author that I suspected of gaming the system. And this is what the stats show on these 10 books (at least 100 reviews) :

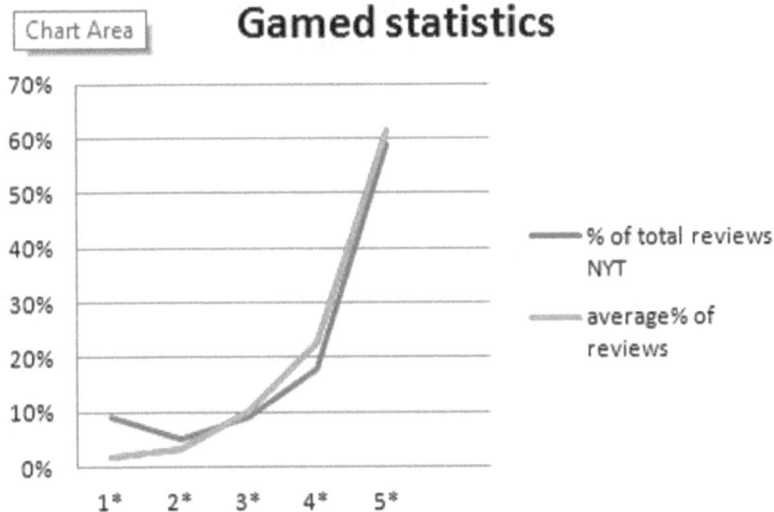

Although the figures seem to line up, when looking closer at the 1* and 2* ratings, it turns out that the 1* rating is now about 2% which is half of that of the top 10 sellers. The 1* and 2* ratings are only 4%. And this is what we would expect. Authors who are gaming the system, will automatically create fake 5* ratings (and maybe some 4*). But that means that some other ratings have to give up something percentage wise.

I repeated this for a couple of other authors and this 'symptom' was confirmed. All of them had a significantly lower 1* and 2* star ratings compared to the top sellers list.

Which drives me finally to the following point: Although these examples seem clear shills, it is very hard to prove for 100% sure that they are. We, human beings, are not very good in detecting fake reviews.

So that is the first problem that Amazon has to cope with. There have been some software developments to detect fake reviews, but their accuracy is still far from perfect. So the only way to do this , is having them verified by human beings.

But as I explained in the earlier chapters, there are TENS OF THOUSANDS of reviews on Amazon every day. So in practice , it is just impossible to screen all reviews by human beings. This explains also why they have the 'report abuse' button next to every review.

We, human beings, are not very good in detecting fake reviews. Researchers found that human beings can identify fake reviews only with an accuracy of around 50%. Which means, not better then the theoretical probability (a chance of 1 out of 2.)

In 2011, Cornwell researchers announced that they had developed software that was able to detect fake reviews.

(http://blogs.cornell.edu/info2040/2011/11/06/information-cascades-the-negative-side-of-positive-reviews/)

However, I haven't found any information if this software is actually used on any sites that use a review system. A study on fake reviews on tripadvisor showed that the software was able to detect fake reviews with an accuracy of almost 90%.

(http://blogs.cornell.edu/info2040/2011/11/06/information-cascades-the-negative-side-of-positive-reviews/)

And although 90% is pretty good, it wasn't clear from the study what the 10% remaining were. If these were 10 fake reviews on 100 that were not identified as such it wouldn't be a big problem. But if the 10% were genuine reviews that were identified as fake, the cure might be worse than the disease.

But there are other cases, where the shill is blatant and for 100% clear. For example, on the same day, 2 reviews on the same book that are EXACTLY , word for word, the same but posted under different names. These are easy to detect by software. So why doesn't Amazon scan for these frauds? Maybe just because it is one on 10.000 times that this happens so maybe they don't consider it worth the development?

But there is a second reason why Amazon might not be in a hurry to get rid of these shills. And that is purely financial.

Suppose that Amazon would have some piece of magical software to eliminate and screen all fake reviews? What would happen?

The top selling books wouldn't be affected. Because they probably don't need fake reviews. And if there are 2 or 3 on a thousand reviews, it wouldn't make any difference. But as we have seen, this is only a very small percentage of the total number of titles. On the long tail side of the sales graph, where we have these thousands of books with something between 0 and 10 reviews, a good part would fall back to 1 review, or maybe even 0.

And even on books that would have 20 reviews, if you take out the 10 fake 5-star reviews and you keep only the 10 real 2 or 3 star reviews, the average would significantly go down.

And as we have seen: Less reviews, fake or real, means less sales. And this would count for ALL products on Amazon. Not just books.

So IF Amazon would have such a magic wand, their sales would significantly be impacted. How much? I have no idea. But don't forget that at the moment of this writing , Amazon is a company that does 75 billion(!) in sales. That's 75.000.000.000.

So suppose that applying this strategy would bring their sales down by 5% . That would be a whopping 3,75 billion dollars. And even if it would be just 1%, it's still a stunning 750 million dollars! So put yourself in the shoes of the Head of Marketing and Sales of Amazon. And one day a company comes along that says:"we have developed some software that will get rid of 100% of all your fake reviews". Would you implement it??? Would your shareholders appreciate such a move??

I cannot answer that question. Because I'm not an Amazon employee and I don't have Amazon stock. But let's say that I would think twice before implementing such a system.

I repeat that, due to the lack of feedback from Amazon, I cannot confirm that these reasons are valid. Amazon states publicly on lots of places on their site that they want to do everything to make a visit to their site a #1 customer experience. And objectively speaking, this would mean: eliminating any trace of suspicious behavior, shills, fake reviews etc. But I have no other proof that they are actually doing this, other than the answer I got "We thoroughly investigate all reports of review abuse".

The downside of fake reviews

The first downside of fake reviews is of course, that they are unethical. They undermine the whole principle of having a voting system that only functions if customer can trust it.

Would you still vote for a president in a democratic country, if you knew that 50% of the votes are bribes? Would you still make a reservation on tripadvisor, based on customer evaluations if you knew that half of them are fake? Would you still buy from an Ebay seller if you discovered that his 99% positive rating was obtained with hundreds of shill accounts?

It is obvious that the average customer will not look as close to reviews as authors and sellers, who have a financial interest in their reviews. Actually, the far majority of customers will probably not even be aware of everything that is going on behind the scenes of reviews.

But as has been proven by several studies, if customers cannot trust the voting system anymore, they will just ignore the reviews, or worse, completely abandon the site.

This problem is not specific to Amazon, but applies to any site that has some kind of evaluation or review system in place.

A recent buzz talked about disappointed travelers who made reservations on tripadvisor, based on customer reviews, which appeared to be fake and posted by scrupulous owners of hotels.

Another drawback of using fake reviews is that the author exposes him/herself to creating an exaggerated positive view of his book, which doesn't correspond with reality. The more highly positive reviews a product has, the higher the expectation is of future buyers regarding the quality of the product. If, after purchase, the product doesn't correspond at all with the high expectation that was created by the fake reviews, the sanction is unavoidable. Returns and negative reviews that can really kill all the sales.

This is also a phenomenon that is common to books that use lots of fake reviews. In the beginning the average rating is high, mainly created by the fake reviews. When the author stops posting fake reviews, the real customer reviews start to trickle in with 1 and 2 star ratings. And the average rating will quickly go down.

And finally, there is the risk that Amazon will close an account. As stated before, I have no proof that they ever did (although suspension happens regularly), but they do state that they have a "zero-tolerance" policy. So think about it: If you have worked for 1, 2 or 3 years to build up your book business, would you put that at stake by using fake reviews for your next book?

I can only answer that question for myself. And every author can make his own judgments if the financial gain is worth the risk.

Which brings me to the question: Is it worth it?

I think I have to distinguish two cases here:

• Your book is good.

In this case, your book WILL sell. Using fake reviews may only speed the process up a little bit. But because your book is good, it would really be a shame when you turn into a bestselling writer and after a while someone finds out that you used fake reviews to bootstrap your career. So my point of view is: If you have a good book, just be patient and sales will come in.

• Your book is not good.

If your book is NOT good (or even very bad), then fake reviews may help to increase sales in the beginning. But fake 5* reviews don't turn a bad book into a good book. So the gain will only be very short term. When real customer feedback comes in, it may be even worse than if you hadn't used fake reviews, because the customer's expectation is much higher.

My conclusion: If your book is NOT good, it will not get better with fake reviews. Sooner or later your book will get hit by unsatisfied customers. So there is only a short period of financial gain.

To summarize, for me there is no real gain to be obtained from fake reviews, besides maybe a short spike in revenues. Every author has to decide what is more important to him. The financial side, or his integrity and honesty.

How to promote your book

This book is not specifically about how to market your eBook. However, we have to distinguish promotion efforts and tactics used to obtain positive reviews.

To promote your book, almost anything is allowed. You may post it on as many sites as you wish. You may spend all the money you like on publicity. You may distribute free copies as many as you want .

Note that you may NOT giveaway your book anywhere for free if your book is part of the KDP select program . In that case, only Amazon may distribute your book(s). Even free downloads.

Here are some things you can do to promote your book :

- Run a free promotion (if your book is subscribed to the KDP select program)

- Run a countdown deal (idem. Part of KDP select)

- Announce your free or countdown promotions on dedicated FB groups. There are dozens and dozens of FB groups with thousands of readers each.

- Announce your promotions on Twitter. If you don't have a large following, you can use a $5 fiverr gig, to get your message posted to a large Twitter following or a number of FB groups.

- Announce your book on free promotion sites

- Announce your book on your own site and write a blog post about it.

- Buy your own books and send them as a gift to potential readers or reviewers. This is part of the Gifting for Kindle program. When readers redeem your gift, this gift will be accounted for just as a regular sale. For more information see Gifting for Kindle.

(https://kdp.amazon.com/help?topicId=A2SPN65RHEW2G)

For a more exhaustive list on how to promote your book, please read my 159 page book 'The Ultimate Kindle Marketing Guide. The Best Collection of Marketing Tactics to Boost Your Sales'.

One word of caution. If you decide to do paid promotions by using keyword auctions (for example a paid FB ad or a Google AdWords campaign), you are NOT allowed to use your Amazon affiliate link to your book. In that case, you should use the general non-affiliate link.

Fake Review Bloopers

To end this book on a more funny tone, I have collected a number of fake review bloopers. Because some people are really clumsy when writing fake reviews and include something that is a clear giveaway that it is a fake.

I haven't copied the reviews word for word, neither the books on which they were posted, because the objective is not to pin point specific books or authors. Just to have a good laugh about the bloopers.

- The reader that doesn't like to read good books : "This book is really a great read. Highly recommended", followed by a 1-star rating.

- The reviewer who doesn't have a lot of time : Publishes 10 reviews for different books in completely different genres, all EXACTLY the same.

- The guy who likes to read uninteresting stuff : "Nothing really interesting in this book". 5-star.

- The father and son who read the same book on the same day: On the same day two 10-line reviews appear which are EXACTLY the same, but posted under different names.

- The guy who reads 50 books a day: Leaves 15 reviews on 15 different books all from the same author on the same day.

- The guy without the spell checker. His books are full with spelling mistakes. Clearly not a native English speaker. All his books have a lot of reviews, all having the same spelling mistakes.

- The new Stephen King. The guy who publishes his fist book and gets 50 5-star reviews in the first 2 days.

- The guy who confuses categories: "Very romantic story. I really liked the girl". 5-star. (A novel about horror without any girl)

- The guy who knows the author VERY well: "This is a GREAT book. The author has spent 40 days writing this book". 5-star

- The guy who does the accounting for the author: "This is really another great book from XXX. This is really a very successful writer. He is selling already X hundred copies A DAY"

- The guy who doesn't know the author: "This was a great read. I didn't know this author. He writes great books, like his wife".

- The guy who hates the genre but buys books in it anyway:"I don't like horror novels. And this one was really bad". 1-star.

- The early bird:"I'm only on page 3 . This is probably not such a great book as I thought it would". 2-star.

- The guy who confuses advertising and review space: 89 reviews all starting with "As the bestselling author of book XYZ, I think..."

- The lady who is forced to read eBooks: "I didn't like this book. I hate reading eBooks anyway". 1-star.

- The guy who does a VERY extensive review of the book. Including the story, the characters, the plot and the ending.

- The totally empty useless review: "This is a good book. I recommend". 5-star (repeated on 50 books).

Top 10 Funny Reviews

In my research, I also bumped on just funny reviews. It was clear that these were written just for fun and that the reviewer didn't really buy the product. Some of these reviews have become real classics and some products have hundreds of these reviews.

Now I have seen heated discussions even on these types of reviews. Because some people say: "Yes, these are funny, BUT.. they are fake, so they should be taken down". And strictly speaking, they are right.

Personally I don't have a problem with these kind of reviews because:

• There aren't thousands and thousands of them. The day that they become 50% of all reviews, maybe Amazon would start doing something about it.

• Yes, they are fake, but the writing and humor makes it very clear that the whole review is nonsense.

• There is no financial gain to be obtained.

• The sales of the product don't get severely impacted by these reviews. Actually I think it is a rather positive effect.

Personally I don't mind about these fake reviews. And the fact that most of them are well-known and still online means that Amazon also doesn't have a problem with these kinds of reviews.

So to finish this book, here is the top 10 list of funny reviews:

<u>**How to Avoid Huge Ships.**</u>

This book has hundreds of hilarious reviews. Here are some of them:

"I live near a park and frequently walk around the local area. Given the amount of dog mess that is on the pavements I thought this book would be the ideal read to stop me having to scrape my shoes on the grass before going home. It was only after it arrived that I looked closely at the title and realised it said 'How to Avoid Huge SHIPS'. A simple error that means I am still treading on massive examples of canine excrement. Having said that, I read the book anyway, and I'm pleased to say I'm not even having near misses with huge ships anymore. No sir, they aint getting anywhere near me!" (3-star)

"I bought How to Avoid Huge Ships as a companion to Captain Trimmer's other excellent titles: How to Avoid a Train, and How to Avoid the Empire State Building. These books are fast paced, well written and the hard won knowledge found in them is as inspirational as it is informational. After reading them I haven't been hit by anything bigger than a diesel bus. Thanks captain!" (5-star).

All reviews on this item are here:

http://www.amazon.com/Avoid-Huge-Ships-John-Trimmer/product-reviews/0870334336/ref=cm_rdp_hist_hdr_cm_cr_acr_txt?ie=UTF8&showViewpoints=1

Sugar Free Haribo Gummi Bears

"Oh man...words cannot express what happened to me after eating these. The Gummi Bear "Cleanse". If you are someone that can tolerate the sugar substitute, enjoy. If you are like the dozens of people that tried my order, RUN!

First of all, for taste I would rate these a 5. So good. Soft, true-to-taste fruit flavors like the sugar variety...I was a happy camper.

BUT (or should I say BUTT), not long after eating about 20 of these all hell broke loose. I had a gastrointestinal experience like nothing I've ever imagined. Cramps, sweating, bloating beyond my worst nightmare. I've had food poisoning from some bad shellfish and that was almost like a skip in the park compared to what was going on inside me.

Then came the, uh, flatulence. Heavens to Murgatroyd, the sounds, like trumpets calling the demons back to Hell...the stench, like 1,000 rotten corpses vomited. I couldn't stand to stay in one room for fear of succumbing to my own odors.

But wait; there's more. What came out of me felt like someone tried to funnel Niagara Falls through a coffee straw. I swear my sphincters were screaming. It felt like my delicate starfish was a gaping maw projectile vomiting a torrential flood of toxic waste. 100% liquid. Flammable liquid. NAPALM. It was actually a bit humorous (for a nanosecond)as it was just beyond anything I could imagine possible.

AND IT WENT ON FOR HOURS."

Read the full review here.

http://www.amazon.com/Haribo-Gummi-Bears-Sugar-Free/dp/B000EVQWKC/ref=cm_rdp_product

The Hutzler 571 Banana Slicer

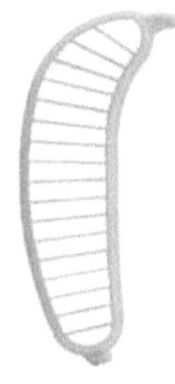

"I tried the banana slicer and found it unacceptable. As shown in the picture, the slices is curved from left to right. All of my bananas are bent the other way."(2-star). "

"I can't believe anyone could be so inept as to think that they couldn't slice their bananas because they bent "the wrong way." All that person has to do is to buy the model 571C Banana Slicer that is for bananas that bend the other way. Although I prefer left-bending bananas, I got both the 571B and the 571C so that when shopping, I don't have to have the hassle of finding bananas with the correct polarity. I hope "Angle Was Wrong" sees the light and removes that harsh one-star rating for this indispensable product duo."

All reviews here.

Three Wolf Moon-T-shirt

"This item has wolves on it which makes it intrinsically sweet and worth 5 stars by itself, but once I tried it on, that's when the magic happened. After checking to ensure that the shirt would properly cover my girth, I walked from my trailer to Wal-mart with the shirt on and was immediately approached by women. The women knew from the wolves on my shirt that I, like a wolf, am a mysterious loner who knows how to 'howl at the moon' from time to time (if you catch my drift!). The women that approached me wanted to know if I would be their boyfriend and/or give them money for something they called mehth. I told them no, because they didn't have enough teeth, and frankly a man with a wolf-shirt shouldn't settle for the first thing that comes to him.

I arrived at Wal-mart, mounted my courtesy-scooter (walking is such a drag!) sitting side saddle so that my wolves would show. While I was browsing tube socks, I could hear aroused asthmatic breathing behind me. I turned around to see a slightly sweaty dream in sweatpants and flip-flops standing there. She told me she liked the wolves on my shirt, I told her I wanted to howl at her moon. She offered me a swig from her mountain dew, and I drove my scooter, with her shuffling along side out the door and into the rest of our lives. Thank you wolf shirt.

*Pros: Fits my girthy frame, has wolves on it, attracts women
Cons: Only 3 wolves (could probably use a few more on the 'guns'),*

cannot see wolves when sitting with arms crossed, wolves would have been better if they glowed in the dark."

All reviews here

http://www.amazon.com/The-Mountain-Three-Short-Sleeve/product-reviews/B002HJ377A/ref=dpx_acr_txt?showViewpoints=1

BIC Cristal For Her Ball Pen

"Someone has answered my gentle prayers and FINALLY designed a pen that I can use all month long! I use it when I'm swimming, riding a horse, walking on the beach and doing yoga. It's comfortable, leak-proof, non-slip and it makes me feel so feminine and pretty! Since I've begun using these pens, men have found me more attractive and approchable. It has given me soft skin and manageable hair and it has really given me the self-esteem I needed to start a book club and flirt with the bag-boy at my local market. My drawings of kittens and ponies have improved, and now that I'm writing my last name hyphenated with the Robert Pattinson's last name, I really believe he may some day marry me! I'm positively giddy. Those smart men in marketing have come up with a pen that my lady parts can really identify with.

Where has this pen been all my life???"

All reviews here

http://www.amazon.com/BIC-Cristal-1-0mm-Black-MSLP16-Blk/product-reviews/B004F9QBE6/ref=cm_cr_dp_qt_see_all_top?ie=UTF8&showViewpoints=1&sortBy=byRankDescending

Denon AKDL1 Dedicated Link Cable

"The cable knew where to go, and hooked itself into the correct ports without help from me."

All reviews here

http://www.amazon.com/Denon-AKDL1-Dedicated-Discontinued-Manufacturer/product-reviews/B000I1X6PM/ref=dpx_acr_txt?showViewpoints=1

Zenith Men's 96.0529.4035/51.M Defy Xtreme Tourbillon Titanium Chronograph Watch

"I wasn't going to buy this watch, but then I noticed Amazon had it with $58,000 off! What a deal. With the money I saved I purchased a brand new BMW and still had money left over for a Disney vacation. How many watches save you money to buy a car and a vacation?

Now whenever I see someone with money troubles I tell them to buy this watch and save $58,000. I am considering buying 10 of these watches so I can save $580,000 and buy a house on cash. Retirement saving is also no longer a concern for me, as I plan to buy one every year and live off the $58,000 I save."

All reviews here.

A Million Random Digits with 100,000 Normal Deviates

"After exploring the "Search Inside This Book" feature and snooping through a few of the embedded prose poems, I knew that this was a book I needed on my shelf. (Though I do admit I ordered it (ostensibly) for my girlfriend's birthday--and borrowed it when she was done!) I finished the tome in one enraptured sitting and, despite a limp third act denouement, the book was taut, well paced, and fresh.

*I do, however, have one concern. I stumbled upon the book while looking up the ISBN number for Haynes' Owner Workshop Manual for Honda 2-valve Twins (1977 - 1985) -- and I got to thinking... Perhaps running across ISBN# 1 85010 359 3 in Rand's "A Million Random Digits" wasn't a coincidence -- perhaps some of the digits aren't that *random* at all. I don't mean to be an alarmist--and I certainly don't bandy about charges of plagiarism lightly--but if you will, please note this excerpt from the author's tender preface:*

738 9377504 03478 47589 43 705 47309 67490 27348 57490 57443509 37405 40978 39794 "31847 57303!" 57049 325740 57403 7509347?

Now, we can't help but notice a completely different "voice" littered throughout the book. For example, in the opening of the penultimate chapter:

704478 489 705 47390 278 574409 3705 978794 9847 57303 57049 32740 574035093 473

Or the crassness in the "bedroom" scene:

473268978 971 23473 3785 [expletive] 3434987 3490809 34709 34908 40700 34087 439874 97835

And after the embarrassment (we'd all rather forget) concerning Wm. T Metzger's otherwise breathtaking "Table of 10,000 square roots: Gives square roots up to 4 digits on the basis of the square roots arranged in consecutive order 1 to 10,000 and the numbers ranging from 1 to 100,000,000" the publishing world can't afford another snafu."

All reviews here

http://www.amazon.com/Million-Random-Digits-Normal-Deviates/product-reviews/0833030477/ref=dp_top_cm_cr_acr_txt?ie=UTF8&show Viewpoints=1

Samsung UN85S9 85-Inch 4K Ultra HD 120Hz 3D Smart LED TV

"My wife and I bought this after selling our daughter Amanda into white slavery. We actually got a refurbished. It's missing the remote, but oh well-- for $10K off, I can afford a universal, right? The picture is amazing. I've never seen the world with such clarity.

Amanda, if you're reading this, hang in there, honey! We'll see you in a year.

*****

I just wanted to add an addendum to my review. Since posting it, we have received a flood of responses. People have said some pretty hurtful things--even questioning our values. Let me assure you, this was not an easy decision to make, and we made it as a family. Obviously, it's very personal. But in light of all the second-guessing, I wanted to explain our thinking.

First and foremost, screen size. I really think you can't go too big. 85" may seem huge, but you get used to it fast. Second, resolution. Is 4K overkill? Please, that's what they said about 1080P! More dots = better. Period. And as far as this being a $40,000 "dumb" TV, people need to re-read my initial post: WE BOUGHT IT REFURBISHED. It was only $30,000.

Some of you may think I'm avoiding the "elephant in the room"-the real reason why this was such a heart-wrenching choice. So let's just get it out there. Yes, the 120 Hz refresh rate is a disappointment, especially on a 4K. But life is full of compromises. And frankly, we hardly notice. All in all, no regrets.

P.S., as for our daughter, NO ONE has the right to question our parenting. Totally out of bounds. Amanda was going into 7th grade, so it was going to be a transitional year anyway. Now she gets to see the world. How many kids her age get to go to Bahrain? I sure as heck didn't, but you don't hear me screaming "child abuse." Bottom line: MYOB! Seriously."

All reviews here: http://www.amazon.com/Samsung-UN85S9-85-Inch-Ultra-120Hz/product-reviews/B00CMEN95U/ref=cm_cr_dp_qt_see_all_top?ie=UTF8&showViewpoints=1&sortBy=byRankDescending

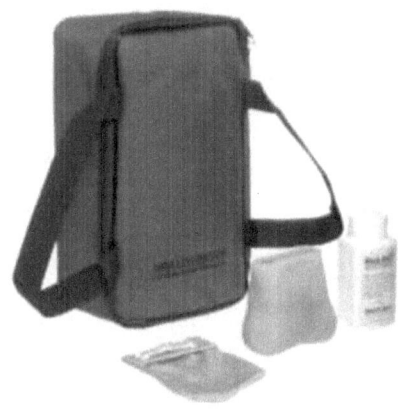

"Who doesn't love playing with scrotum? I know I do! So does my wife. But sometimes I have to leave the house to, I don't know, go to work or buy groceries and I have to take my scrotum away from my wife's hands. This made her sad... until NOW! Now she has a scrotum to play with when I'm not around. I also find it useful when I feel the need to play with a scrotum other than my own and don't want to impose on coworkers, friends, family members (I said 'members') or our local priest.

Now the priest is sad. Oh well, I'm more than happy with my new rubber scrotum... a must have!"

All reviews here :

http://www.amazon.com/3B-Scientific-W43014-Testicle-Self/product-reviews/B005OSVZN4/ref=pr_all_summary_cm_cr_acr_txt?ie=UTF8&showViewpoints=1&sortBy=bySubmissionDateDescending

Conclusion

Fake reviews will exist, as long as there is financial gain to be obtained by using them. Certain authors just don't care about the ethical side.

Despite that observation, I think that if you are seriously working on a long term career as a trusted author, there is only one way to go. Play it by the rules. Using unethical tactics will deserve everyone. The honest writers, the websites, and finally in the long run, the cheating author himself.

Voting systems will only work, if customers can trust that the votes are genuine. If the voting system becomes skewed in a significant way, customers will abandon and everyone will lose.

I don't have a ready-made solution for this problem, other than recommending fellow authors to play it by the rules. And IF your book is good, it WILL sell.

I have never signaled a shill, simply because I prefer spending my time on writing, rather than unmasking fake reviews. The only one who can do something about it, is Amazon.

Unfortunately, and despite my request, I haven't obtained any response from Amazon themselves on the subject. But it is for sure that they are aware of the problem.

I have always been convinced that honesty will pay off on the long term, and there is no reason for me to make an exception on this regarding my books.

Every author has to decide for himself what he finds acceptable and where his limits of ethical behavior are. I hope that this book will help aspiring authors to form themselves an opinion about the use of fake reviews.

The only advice I can give you:

Keep writing!!

Thank you

Thank you for having read my book till the end. I hope you liked it and that you have learned what you were looking for.

If you have appreciated my book I would like to ask you just ONE favor. Please leave me an honest review on Amazon by going here

http://www.amazon.com/dp/B00LNMY0VO

If you got this book for free during a promotion period, I would highly appreciate it if you could leave me an honest review.

It will only take you a minute or two. I value any feedback from you. If it is really positive, I have attained my objective of adding real value in my book for you. If it is average or less, I can use your feedback to make it better.

I wish you lots of success in your online activities.

Timo

About the Author

Biography

Timo is a writer, blogger and IT expert. He writes about complex things, like keyword research, affiliate marketing and online marketing. But in a language that is understandable for everybody.

He uses 30+ years experience in computers, networking, hardware, software, development, internet, marketing, sales and online business to teach others how to grasp complex issues. His international experience, working abroad in several European countries, US and Africa has given him a broad view on different cultures and civilizations.

He has followed the development of the internet right from the start. In the 80's just with email and private networks, and from the early 90's onwards he was one of the first ones to work with the first websites.

Learn from the author how to setup an online business, how to understand everything about search engines, how to create your own 'internet life-style'.

His books are extremely results-oriented: You are looking for a solution to a specific problem? When you read a book from the author, you will find the answer.

In straight-to-the-point explanations without the fluff.

When Timo is not writing or blogging he spends his time on the magnificent beaches between St Tropez and Monaco, relaxing in a pub in Cannes, playing chess or travelling to his home country : The Netherlands.

All Books from the Author

Here are all my books:

- How to Find Niche Markets that Sell. A complete Guide to Niche Marketing Resources. Available for FREE on my website http://www.onlinemoneyexplained.com

- 150 Ways to Make Money Online. Learn How to Make Hard Cash with Your Computer from Home

- Find Golden Keywords with FREE software. Dig up Golden Nuggets with Google Keyword Planner.

- The Ultimate Kindle Formatting Guide. From Word to Kindle. Better Formatting = More Sales

- How to Make Money with eBooks. The Best Collection of Marketing Tactics to Boost Your Sales.

- Amazon Reviews Exposed. The Truth about Amazon Reviews.

- The Complete Book Cover Creation Guide. What makes a good cover and how to create your own for FREE.

- How to Make Book Covers that Sell. Everything You Need to Know About Book Cover Design. (Part I of The Complete Book Cover Creation Guide).

- How to Create Professional Book Covers. Make Your Own Free Book Covers Free With GIMP. (Part II of The Complete Book Cover Creation Guide)

www.ingramcontent.com/pod-product-compliance
Lightning Source LLC
Chambersburg PA
CBHW030703190526
45164CB00004B/339